SPOT

MOTORSPORTS

INDY CARS

by Alissa Thielges

amicus LEARNING

speedway

front wing

Look for these words and pictures as you read.

steering wheel

tire

Indy cars are fast race cars.

Vroom!

Look at them go!

See the speedway?
It is a big, round track.
The longest race is 200 laps.

speedway

See the car grid?
Indy cars line up there.
The race is about to start.

MCLAUGHLIN

front wing

See the front wing?
It pushes the air down.
It keeps the car steady.

Service
24
Service
MERCHANDISE
Garrard
ELECTRONICS
PEPSI
PPG
BOSCH
HOLSET
HOLSET
IBM
DieHard
BOSCH

steering wheel

See the steering wheel?
It has a lot of buttons.
One makes the car go faster.

PLC
P2P
P2P
REV LIMIT
PAGE
MIXTURE
NEUTRAL
REVERSE
RESET

See the tires?
They are smooth.
They help the car go fast.

tire

HMD

It is the final lap.
A flag drops.
We have a winner!

speedway

front wing

Did you find?

steering wheel

tire

Spot is published by Amicus Learning, an imprint of Amicus
P.O. Box 227, Mankato, MN 56002
www.amicuspublishing.us

Library of Congress Cataloging-in-Publication Data
Names: Thielges, Alissa, 1995- author.
Title: Indy cars / by Alissa Thielges.
Description: Mankato, MN : Amicus Learning, [2026] | Series: Spot motorsports | Audience: Ages 4–7 | Audience: Grades K–1 | Summary: "Indy cars are race cars named after the Indianapolis (Indy) 500, a 500-lap race in Indiana. The cars have wings and an open cockpit. This search-and-find book reinforces new vocabulary words with simple facts and compelling photographs to teach kindergarten readers about motorsports"– Provided by publisher.
Identifiers: LCCN 2024050075 (print) | LCCN 2024050076 (ebook) | ISBN 9798892004831 (library binding) | ISBN 9798892005371 (paperback) | ISBN 9798892005913 (ebook)
Subjects: LCSH: Indy cars–Juvenile literature. |Automobiles, Racing–Juvenile literature. | CYAC: Indy cars. | Automobiles, Racing.
Classification: LCC TL236.25 .T45 2026 (print) | LCC TL236.25 (ebook) | DDC 629.228/5–dc23/eng/20241219
LC record available at https://lccn.loc.gov/2024050075
LC ebook record available at https://lccn.loc.gov/2024050076

Ana Brauer, editor
Deb Miner, series designer
Sara Hood, book designer and photo researcher

Photos by Alamy Stock Photo/Kirby Lee, 4–5; Forrest Bowman III, 10–11; Getty Images/Brian Spurlock/Icon Sportswire, 6–7, David Allio/Icon Sportswire, 3, Fred Vuich, 14, Pascal Rondeau, 8–9; Shutterstock/Grindstone Media Group, cover, 1, 12–13